GIANT DINOSAURS

by ERNA ROWE pictures by MERLE SMITH

SCHOLASTIC BOOK SERVICES NEW YORK · TORONTO · LONDON · AUCKLAND · SYDNEY

ISBN: 0-590-30927-7

12 11 10 9 8 7 6 5 4 3 2 1   10   9/7 0 1 2 3 4/8

Printed in the U.S.A.   02

To Wayne, John, Tommy, Gordon and Ambrozio,

who wanted to know more about dinosaurs,

especially big ones.

Dinosaurs were giants that lived long, long ago.

There were all sorts of giant dinosaurs.

Trachodon

(TRACK — oh — don)

Trachodon was as big as a house.

His bill

looked like a duck's

so he is also called DUCKBILL.

He was a plant eater.

Trachodon had 2,000 teeth!

Brontosaurus

(BRON — to — SOR — us)

His name means
"Thunder Lizard."
When he walked,
it sounded like
thunder.

He lived on plants too.

Brontosaurus was as big as two school rooms.

Brachiosaurus

(BRAK — ee — oh — SOR — us)

lived in water.

He weighed more than any other dinosaur.

He was as heavy as ten elephants!

Diplodocus

(Di — PLOD — oh — kus)

was as long as five or six cars.

He was the **LONGEST** dinosaur ever to live on earth.

Tyrannosaurus Rex

(Ti — RAN — oh — SOR — us)

could run very fast.

He was as tall as a telephone pole.
He was the King of the dinosaurs.

Tyrannosaurus was a meat eater.

He attacked plant eaters.

He was very fierce.

His teeth were long and sharp!

Stegosaurus

(STEG — oh — SOR — us)

was a plant eater.
The plates on his back and the spikes on his
tail helped protect him from meat eaters.

Stegosaurus would fit in a living room!

He was smaller than the other giant dinosaurs.

Triceratops

(Try — SER — a — tops)

lived on plants too.

He had two sharp horns on his head and another on his nose.

Would a meat eater attack Triceratops?

Baby dinosaurs came from eggs.

Some of these eggs have been found after millions of years. They have turned to stone.

Dinosaurs made huge footprints in the mud.
Some are as long as your arm.
After a long, long, long time, the mud became
hard and turned to stone. Today you can see
dinosaur footprints in a museum.

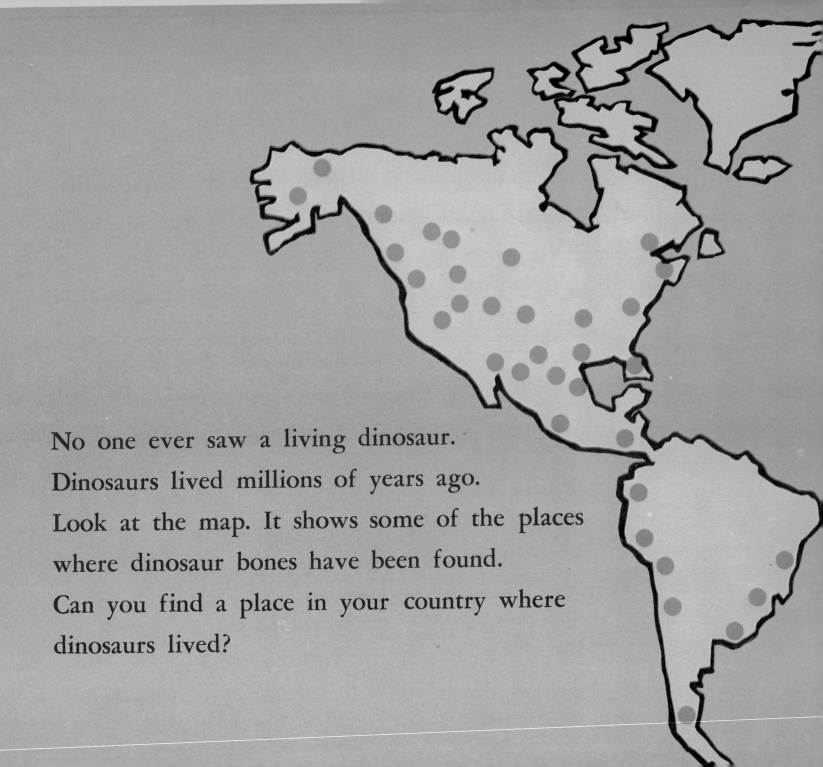

No one ever saw a living dinosaur.

Dinosaurs lived millions of years ago.

Look at the map. It shows some of the places
where dinosaur bones have been found.

Can you find a place in your country where
dinosaurs lived?

If you want to learn more about dinosaurs,
you can go to a museum.

Here is a skeleton of a Brontosaurus in a museum.
It will make you feel very small.

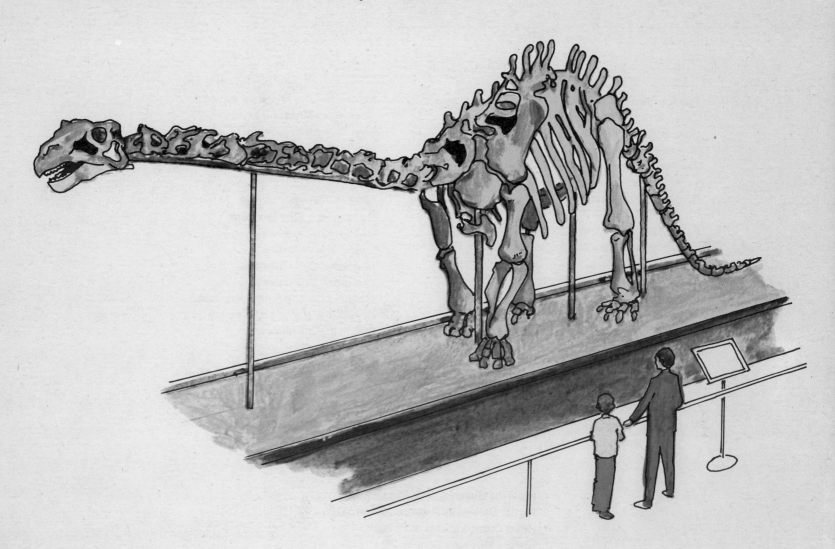

Many museums have displays about dinosaurs.

You can see displays at these museums:

UNITED STATES

The American Museum of Natural History, New York City, NY.

United States Natural History Museum, Smithsonian Institution, Washington, D.C.

Peabody Museum of Natural History, Yale University, New Haven, CT.

Carnegie Museum of the Natural Sciences, Pittsburgh, PA.

Field Museum of Natural History, Chicago, IL.

The Academy of Natural Sciences of Philadelphia, Philadelphia, PA.

Pratt Museum of Geology, Amherst College, Amherst, MA.

Museum of Paleontology, University of Michigan, Ann Arbor, MI.

University of Nebraska Museum, Lincoln, NE.

Geological Museum of Utah, University of Utah, Salt Lake City, UT.

Museum of Comparative Zoology, Harvard University, Cambridge, MA.

Museum of Paleontology, University of California, Berkeley, CA.

UNITED KINGDOM

Natural History Museum, London.

Geological Museum, London.

Royal Scottish Museum, Edinburgh.

University Museum, Oxford.

Sedgewick Museum, Cambridge.

Local museums:

Birmingham, **City Museum.**

Bristol, **City Museum.**

Leeds, **City Museum.**

Leicester, **City Museum.**

Liverpool, **City Museum.**

Manchester, **University Museum.**

Newcastle, **Hancock Museum,** Newcastle University.

Sheffield, **City Museum.**

AUSTRALIA

Australian Museum, Sydney.

Queensland Museum, Brisbane.

South Australian Museum, Adelaide.

West Australian Museum, Perth.

CANADA

National Museum of Canada, Ottawa.

McGill University Museum, Montreal.

Royal Ontario Museum, Toronto.

History Museum, Regina.

Some dinosaurs were small. But all of the dinosaurs in this book were GIANTS. This chart shows the size of all the dinosaurs in this book.

BRONTOSAURUS

BRACHIOSAURUS

STEGOSAURUS

DIPLODOCUS

TRICERATOPS

TYRANNOSAURUS

TRACHODON

Feet | 10 | 20 | 30 | 40 | 50 | 60 | 70 | 80 | 90 | 100

Meters | 10 | 20 | 30